Refuel Your Wait

Refuel Your Wait

Find Hope and Overcome Fear While Adopting

Laci Richter

RESOURCE *Publications* · Eugene, Oregon

REFUEL YOUR WAIT
Find Hope and Overcome Fear While Adopting

Resource Publications
An Imprint of Wipf and Stock Publishers
199 W. 8th Ave., Suite 3
Eugene, OR 97401

www.wipfandstock.com

PAPERBACK ISBN: 978-1-7252-7526-3
HARDCOVER ISBN: 978-1-7252-7527-0
EBOOK ISBN: 978-1-7252-7528-7

Manufactured in the U.S.A.   09/04/20

To all those who are waiting.

Contents

Contents

Contents

Preface

REFUEL YOUR WAIT IS the story of how I was able to find hope and peace in the process of becoming a parent through adoption.

As a girl from South Louisiana my well-meaning family was alarmed at the fact that I remained single and unspoken for as I quickly approached the age of thirty. Thankfully, in early 2005, just in the nick of time, I stumbled upon and met the man who quickly became my husband. We had a whirlwind courtship that included a move across the country after a year into our relationship. My family also became alarmed at this move with no sign of a wedding ring on my finger. In 2008, we married and my well-meaning family became my husband's well-meaning family also.

In 2010, after appreciating life as a couple with plenty of travel, abundant excursions, and generous dinners at nice restaurants, we decided it was time to start a family. In 2012, after one year of trying to conceive naturally and then one year of fertility treatments, we chose to move on to the adoption process. We had discussions early in our marriage that if we couldn't conceive for any reason we would adopt. Some of our very dear friends had built their family by adoption and we mistakenly thought we knew a bit about the process. It was a natural and easy decision for us.

It was during our adoption wait that God decided to speak directly to me. As he and I were early on in our relationship, it took me some time to recognize his voice. I imagined God's voice would be a scary and booming sound cutting through silence. And I have to tell you, prior to my personal experience, if someone claimed they were spoken to by God, I probably stopped listening pretty quickly. But then I heard him, and his voice wasn't weird or scary or booming.

My Heavenly Father, who knows me very well, spoke to me delicately and gracefully. Early one morning in the fall of 2012, I awoke from a dream with a specific date lingering in my thoughts. The date was April 10. I remember no other details of the dream besides the specific date and my deceased grandfather being present. I searched my memory to find the significance of the date as it may pertain to my grandfather, but it didn't. I almost discarded the thought but decided to journal about it instead. You know, in case God was speaking to me. I shared the experience with my husband and a few close friends. After a while, the experience started to fade away as life and the waiting continued.

About six months later on April 9, 2013, we received the call that every adoptive family is impatiently waiting for. That call was our agency telling us about an expectant mother who was making an adoption plan and wanted to meet us. And on April 10–the date in my dream–we met the woman who chose us to parent her unborn child. God spoke to me with a dream, a date, and confirmation that this was the child we would parent. It would be a long seventeen weeks before the baby was born and the expectant mother's decision was final. Even with this confirmation from my Heavenly Father, the waiting experience was a test of faith.

Refuel Your Wait is our story of a challenging waiting season filled with many fears along with the Scriptures that personally gave me hope and ultimately joy.

Acknowledgements

To my daughters' birth parents. Our wait was nothing compared to the decisions you chose to make in what was most likely the toughest season of your lives. To put your child's future and well-being above your own by placing them for adoption was painful and courageous. I am reminded of your grief and your pride running through my home on a daily basis.

To my daughters, even though I have to remind you every morning that you are not allowed in my writing office, I love hearing your little feet come down the stairs and head directly toward me. I pray you have memories of morning snuggles in front of my computer and know that I was working on sharing the story of how you joined our family.

To my husband, Robbie, thank you for being the leader of "Team Richter." I appreciate your technical support but more importantly your family support. You are the smartest, funniest, most composed person I know. Just having you in the room with me brings me peace and creativity.

To my fellow author, mentor, editor and friend, Damaris, without your experience and words of encouragement this book may have sat on my computer for another three years. Thank you for reviewing my words so that I could experience a preview of how my readers would receive them.

To my friends, Tammie and Brad, without your demands for a book after every word I posted online, this book may have sat in my head or in my notebook forever.

Acknowledgements

To my Alabama Bible study group, without your lessons about the Holy Spirit's role in my life I may have ignored the nudge to journal the process.

Introduction

Courage [kur-ij] *noun* the quality of mind and spirit that enables a person to face difficulty, danger, pain, etc., without fear; bravery.

THE MAJORITY OF OUR lives we are waiting for something. We wait for the right job, a suitable partner, a successful pregnancy, an appropriate move, a timely friendship. We wait for phone calls and emails. We wait for the healing of a loved one or ourselves. We wait for pain to pass and grief to resign. We wait for conventional happiness and expected joy. Because our lives surround waiting, it is important to decide how we will wait. We can choose to wait in fear or we can choose to wait with hope.

When we use the wisdom of a bigger picture to guide our daily interactions and prayer, we choose to wait in courage. We can choose to spin in worry of details that are out of our control. Or we can choose to surrender our wait to the mercy of God's promises. His Word and promises will fill us up and renew our strength and energy with exactly what we need. And when we find ourselves empty again, we will cry out for more strength, more peace, more of his fatherly love. If and when we seek more, he will provide what we need. Because God is our constant and because he is our endless supply of a merciful and gracious love. We can reach for his love and be refilled and refueled every day.

I was called to write this devotion during a challenging season of waiting on my prayers to be answered. My husband and I desperately wanted to become parents and were struggling to do so. The Scriptures, personal stories, and journaling questions are a way to use God's promises to lead you to faith in the waiting. My hope is that you use this devotion in any way that motivates and inspires you to wait with more hope and less fear.

Part One

Wait with Hope

Chapter One

What Are You Waiting For?

"But those who trust in the Lord will find new strength.
They will soar on wings like eagles; they will run and
not grow weary; they will walk and not faint."

(ISAIAH 40:31 NLT)

OUR LIVES ARE FILLED with waiting. At every moment we are waiting for a job, a phone call, an email, a relationship, medical results, healing. There are so many moments of waiting that we might expect to get better at waiting. Conceivably, we could become more patient while waiting. Or maybe we could become more productive during the wait.

When my husband and I entered the adoption process, we traded in waiting for doctor appointments and refills of prescriptions for a different kind of waiting. We were now waiting for our home study to be complete, background checks to clear, and our profile to be shown. We were waiting to be matched with an expectant parent, for the baby to be born, for the revocation period to pass, and for a court date to finalize the adoption. So much waiting can be paralyzing for a person. In some of the earlier moments, I did nothing else but sit and wait. Once I realized that the Lord gives purpose to a wait, I was able to lean into him, to seek him, to need him, while I waited.

When we wait on the Lord, he will continually renew our strength, supply our patience, and refuel our energy. Just when we think we can't endure one more moment of waiting that is when we will find him. He will show up, pick us up, and push us forward. Because we are all waiting on something at any given moment, we cannot let wait paralyze us. Joyful moments exist within the wait, but we must be actively looking for them.

Wait with Hope

Big or small, list three things you are currently waiting for and how long you have been waiting for them.

Which of these items has stalled your daily production or stolen your daily joy?

What are some ways you can add joy to your wait? (reach out to a friend for support, join a prayer group or Bible study, go on a mini vacation, start a workout plan)

Make a specific plan to intentionally add joy while waiting on these things.

Chapter Two

Change of Plans

"You can make many plans but the Lord's purpose will prevail."

(PROVERBS 19:21)

MOST OF US HAVE a planned timeline for our lives. Those timelines do not include things like health issues, infertility, divorce, accidents, depression, or the loss of a loved one. But our lives include one, if not more than one, major trial. And our lives will not follow the timeline we imagine.

I thought I would be married with children by thirty. My plan did not include a major breakup in my late twenties or a struggle with infertility in my thirties. But the bigger picture did include those trials and more. This path also led me to an amazing man to marry and two incredible children to parent.

Every time I picked up a negative pregnancy test, I made a new plan. Every time we were matched with expectant parents, I made a new plan. Every time we experienced an interrupted adoption, I made a new plan. These plans were meant to bring me purpose and peace. But these plans brought much work and worry and stole much joy.

You will find yourself making plans while waiting. A plan for every scenario possible. Too many plans. Too much worry. The purpose of your planning is to ease your mind and be prepared. But in reality the planning will cause you more stress than necessary. Release the unnecessary planning and surrender to God because his purpose will prevail in every single detail.

Wait with Hope

How is your life different than you planned?

List specific occurrences that you are sure are the Lord's purpose.

Which parts of your life are you still wondering about when it comes to purpose and timing?

Pray specifically to release the planning and control over these areas and hand them over to the Lord's purpose.

Chapter Three

Seasons of Sorrow

"I have told you all this so that you may have peace in me.
Here on earth you will have many trials and sorrows.
But take heart, because I have overcome the world."

(JOHN 16:33)

I EXPERIENCED A HAPPY, simple, and peaceful childhood void of many trials or tragedies. My parents were happily married as far as I knew and still are. My relationship with my siblings is built on love and acceptance. There were no major health issues or shocking accidents. We lost my grandfather when he was in his fifties, but as a young child I thought this was normal. In my teen and young adult years, I faced some losses, the deaths of a couple of friends, and made a few bad decisions but nothing that altered my path.

In my late twenties I met my husband and after a brief romance we moved to California to explore life, further our careers, and become husband and wife. I was oblivious to the fact that my previous journey was relatively stress-free until my husband and I decided to start our family. The next few years were filled with many hard decisions, multiple trials, and some unexpected grief. After a decade of trying to conceive and trying to adopt, we have now moved on from what I call the "waiting season." We are now in the "parenting small children and maintaining a healthy marriage" season (my next book perhaps). We have definitely made it through a hard season, but I cannot expect that life will be untroubled.

We are never guaranteed an easy path. We are actually warned that there will be many trials and sorrows. But if we can arm ourselves with the truth that Jesus has overcome the world, we are assured that we can overcome multiple trials and deep sorrow with our Heavenly Father's peace.

Wait with Hope

List your major trials and sorrows thus far in life. Were you in a relationship with God when you faced those trials?

Are you expecting or preparing for any trials in the immediate future? (loss of an ailing loved one, financial hardship, change in relationship status)

When you are in a season of trials are you aware of God's presence making your path straight, or do you find yourself lost in sorrow?

What action items can you put in place to be near to his word when facing stressful situations? (reading scripture, speaking with faith-filled friends, focusing on prayer life)

Chapter Four

Search and Rescue

"The Lord is good to those who depend on him, to those who search
for him. So it is good to wait quietly for salvation from the Lord."

(LAMENTATIONS 3: 25–26)

FOR ONE YEAR MY husband and I tried unsuccessfully to get pregnant the "good-old-fashioned way." We had an early intuition that something wasn't quite right so we sought medical help right away. Simultaneously, at that one year mark, we were relocating across the country for a job opportunity for my husband.

After the move, we immediately found a specialist and started fertility treatments. During treatments, you are required to spend a lot of time in a doctor's office for weekly ultrasounds and blood work. My husband and I decided that I would take a sabbatical from work while building our family. We did not expect the process of building our family to take three years. During this time, I felt societal pressure to find a job, but I also felt stronger prompts keeping me home.

My time off was intended to be focused on organizing my home and preparing for a child. This preparation time turned into a trying time of failed fertility treatments and several interrupted adoptions. Unexpectedly, that waiting time resulted in a space in which I was searching and developing a personal relationship with God. We quickly found a church that we were comfortable in and we began building a church family. I found God bringing many relationships to me with people of abundant faith and hearts of service. Quiet moments felt uncomfortable and a waste of time, but soon enough my idle time turned into space to think, pray, and write.

Our Heavenly Father rejoices in our dependence on him. The days when we throw our hands in the air and proclaim, "Help me Lord" are music to his ears. He wants us to depend on him, search for him, and yes, wait for him.

Wait with Hope

How often do you make or take time to wait quietly?

What "time wasters" could you eliminate to make space in your day to wait quietly?

Commit to a week with daily quiet time and journal your thoughts.

Chapter Five

Joyful Source

"I pray that God, the source of hope, will fill you completely
with joy and peace because you trust in him. Then you will overflow
with confident hope through the power of the Holy Spirit."

(ROMANS 15:13)

THE YEAR THAT MY husband and I decided to seek fertility treatment was the same year we decided to relocate our lives. We were
living in a city across the country from our families'. We felt the
need to be closer to family and closer to the places where we grew
up as we thought about raising children. My husband's company
had a convenient location near our family with a job opportunity
available for him. After moving across the country and finding a
specialist to work with, we immediately started fertility treatments.
After one year of unsuccessful fertility treatments, we moved
forward to the adoption process. During these years, I remained
unemployed for various reasons which left me with abundant time
for projects and daydreaming of our future family.

After one year stretched into two, I decided it might be better to spend my time doing more than planning a baby nursery
and daydreaming of a family. Through our church, I randomly
fell into a volunteer position for a nonprofit kitchen that provided

meals to the working poor and homeless. With very little industrial kitchen experience or experience with the homeless–this was out of my comfort zone.

While volunteering on a regular basis, I met a group of people whose source of joy was surely that of the Lord. Regardless of the task they had been given, whether it was mopping the floor or serving food, they did the task with complete joy. From the nonprofit leader to the kitchen managers to the servers, every one of them presented with a mysterious shining light. After a few weeks, I was given a consistent task of rolling out the pizza dough for the lunch menu. For two to three hours at a time, I would stand in the same spot and roll out 40 pizzas. It was the most meditative, joyful, fulfilling hours of my week. The people we were serving usually walked in looking defeated yet left in an entirely different light. The meals were about so much more than providing food to those in need. The meals provided nourishment of the spirit and the soul.

God is our source of hope, our source of wisdom, our source of love. The more we trust in him, the more he provides. When we surround ourselves with those who have accepted him as their nourishment, we are then filled with their light. That nourishment, that light that you receive, will then radiate joy and peace towards others.

Wait with Hope

Can you think of a person or a group of people who exude confident hope and joy in their daily actions?

Do you recognize their source of joy as their relationship with God or some other source?

Are there times when you feel drawn to them and other times when you feel the need to avoid them?

Can you think of a place or event that you can find people who radiate this source?

Can you think of daily actions that can bring you closer to people with this source?

Chapter Six

Baby Steps

"We can make our plans, but the Lord determines our steps."

(PROVERBS 16:9)

MY HUSBAND AND I are not high school sweethearts and didn't live in the same state during college. We met when we were twenty-eight and well into the adulthood of finding a permanent job, a better place to live, and mature friends. We enjoyed our dating stage into our newlywed stage and before we knew it, we were thirty-years-old. Now, we were ready to start a family and parent together.

After trying to conceive on our own for a year, we sought help from a doctor. We found a specialist and began the rigorous and exhausting attempt of conceiving through medical intervention and fertility treatments.

At the beginning of each cycle, I would calculate the expected due date of the baby were that fertility treatment to be successful. Then, I would continue on to prepare plans for the future. I would daydream about exactly how we would tell our family the exciting news. I would get wrapped up in decor, colors, and furniture shopping for the nursery. And I would think through what daily life as a stay-at-home mom, with a precious newborn, would look like.

These vivid daydreams consumed my thoughts. Every negative pregnancy test consumed my joy.

I planned for a baby and my Heavenly Father did too; however, our steps and our timeline were not the same. My actions, daydreams, joy, and grief would have changed dramatically had I known it would take four years before my timeline and my Heavenly Father's timeline aligned.

We will have plans and timelines for our lives. But if we seek God for direction of the next steps, then our plans will align, making a more peaceful journey along the way. Disappointments and failures will be on our path, so growing deeper in our relationship with God will help us acknowledge that it is he who determines the ultimate timeline.

Wait with Hope

List one short-term or long-term goal that you are trying to accomplish.

What is your plan and timeline for getting there?

Take one step at a time and prayerfully consult your Heavenly Father on the next step. Do you feel peace? Then keep going. Do you feel a closed door? Reconsider other options and steps.

Chapter Seven

Path of Least Control

"Show me the right path, O Lord; point out the road for me to follow.
Lead me; by your trust and teach me, for you are the God
who saves me. All day long I put my hope in you."

(PSALM 25:4–5)

THE HARDEST PART FOR me when we hit this "infertility bump in the road" was that I had absolutely no control over the issue. I tried to take control by eating the things I should, taking the supplements suggested, and seeking medical treatment, but none of this worked. When we left the fertility efforts behind and started our adoption journey, I felt relief in knowing this process was something more in my control; or so I thought.

When we started the adoption process, I wanted to proceed with the easiest and shortest route. I read all the books and planned our course of action. We signed up with an adoption agency for support and education while we simultaneously worked with adoption lawyers to cover all our bases and quickly get our profile to expectant mothers. Each time an opportunity came our way, I would try to take it, make it mine, and make it work.

Multiple times we faced situations that were not ideal and led to a closed door. These closed doors came in the form of an expectant mother who miscarried before we met her and an expectant mother, whom we met and connected with, but chose another family. There was also an expectant mother who chose us then changed her mind one week before birth. It took almost a year in that process before I realized I was trying too hard to remain in control.

God's path may not always be the easy path or the short path, but it is the straight path. We have many paths available with forks in the road, uphill struggles, and downhill battles. Our Heavenly Father is waiting to guide us in the right direction. He does not promise an easy and painless journey, but he does promise to lead us and make our paths straight.

Wait with Hope

Is there a particular part of your journey in which you continue to try the easy or short path?

What sorts of things are getting in your way on this path?

Prayerfully consider another path, that although may seem longer, may be blessed and straightened by God.

Chapter Eight

Spring Forward

"His righteousness will be like a garden in early spring,
with plants springing up everywhere."

(ISAIAH 61:11)

IN THE SPRING OF 2012, after a long winter of medical procedures and negative pregnancy tests, we were at a crossroads. We needed to decide if we would continue infertility treatments or enter the adoption process.

While we were trying to grow our family, my husband and I busied ourselves with many home projects. One beautiful spring morning we were working in our garden and enjoying the warm sunshine. Our job that day was to transfer our fragile seedlings from egg cartons into the lush garden spot we prepared for them. My husband had meticulously cared for these seedlings indoors for months and now it was time to place them outside. I looked down into my hands holding one tiny healthy green plant. I carefully dug a small hole and placed it into the soil. A feeling of peace and confirmation fell over me. To choose to adopt would mean an expectant mother would plant, grow, and care for her baby until it was time for us to become parents. At that very moment I knew we were ready to move forward in our journey. So we entered a new season of waiting.

Any change can bring hope after a long and challenging season of waiting. A change in month or week, a change in weather or season, a change in schedule or activity. All of these things can refresh and renew our spirit. Look for changes around you and let them give you energy to push forward one more step in your journey.

Wait with Hope

List some activities that renew your spirit and give you hope. (spending time with friends, gardening, painting)

Plan out some activities this week that give you hope.

Schedule these activities on a calendar.

Chapter Nine

Every Little Step

"Your word is a lamp to guide my feet and a light for my path."
(PSALMS 119:105)

AFTER MAKING THE DECISION and expectantly moving forward into the adoption process, we eagerly approached the path. However, we were decelerated by the mountain of paperwork to be completed and a number of mandatory "to do's" to be checked off. Any person wanting to adopt must complete, not only a lengthy application, but a state mandated "home study" conducted by a licensed social worker. The home study is used to prepare, evaluate, and collect information about the family. It is a rigorous process including several in-person meetings and can take months to complete. There is nothing fast or easy about this process.

The home study evaluation requires a person to face and make decisions about their future that expecting parents would never think twice about. I was overwhelmed and disheartened knowing that these were not choices we would have to make if I were pregnant. What race are you open to adopting? What medical issues are you willing to accept? What type of relationship do you want with the birth parents? What states are you willing to travel to? What expenses are you willing to pay? There are so many unknowns which make these decisions very difficult. Some of the toughest decisions to make will not be relevant in the long run; some are vast forks in the road and some are mere steps on a path. But each of these decisions has to be made in the midst of uncertainty and prior to proceeding in the adoption process. For each decision I was struggling with, I would express my concerns to my husband and close friends and then ask for their thoughts. I would then bring my concerns to God through prayer and journaling. Giving attention and time to our values helped us make the best decision we could make with the information we had.

Whether you are facing a major fork in the road or just a minor step on the path, seek his word for guidance. His word will guide your feet one step at a time. Do not look ahead or down the path. Do not try to make more than one decision at a time. Just take one step. Pray. Now take another. We need his guidance. We need his light. We need his word.

Wait with Hope

What fork in the road or decision are you currently facing?

Are you looking too far ahead to make that decision? Back up and identify the first decision to be made.

Consider praying, waiting for peace, and then taking one step. Continue to do this (pray, wait, step) until you have reached your destination. Use this space to pray, wait, step, and journal along the path.

Part Two

Wait with Prayer

Chapter Ten

All the Prayers

"Don't worry about anything; instead pray about everything. Tell
God what you need, and thank him for all he has done."

(PHILIPPIANS 4:6)

I WENT THROUGH A significant prayer season in my life when we
were trying to start our family. I prayed hard, relentlessly, and multiple times a day. I gave thanks because I should, but mostly I was
asking for things and possibly even begging.

After my really "big" prayers during infertility, *God please
let me be pregnant,* and during adoption, *God please let this birth
mother pick us,* I assumed I was all out of prayers. I thought, surely
after those intense years of praying–or more like begging–my
Heavenly Father was nearing his listening and answering quota
with me. And even if I did have prayers left, I should probably
start budgeting them and leaving some of the smaller things off the
table–*God, please don't let me catch this stomach bug from my kids.*
I was never taught this but for some reason I thought that each
person had a limit, and once we reached that limit we were all on
our own. Oh how wrong I was!

One day I was having a discussion in my Bible study group
with a much older and wiser friend about my misconceived notion

of prayer limits. She told me that our God is a limitless God. She also informed me that no prayer is too small. None. You can bring anything and everything to God and you can bring it multiple times. You never ever run out of prayer allowance. He collects all of your big and small prayers and stores them for the right time. God has no limits. Hallelujah.

Bring your small prayers and bring your big prayers. Bring every worry to him. God wants you to worry about nothing and pray about everything. And then thank him.

Wait with Prayer

List your "small" prayers that you keep to yourself. Make it a point to start bringing these to God.

List your big prayers that you take straight to God. Keep taking those to him every day.

Take one day and commit to bringing every big and small thing to God. Pray about any worry and every worry that surfaces in your day. How did this feel and how did it change your day?

Chapter Eleven

Sunrise Surrender

"The Lord is good to those who depend on him, to those who search for him. So it is good to wait quietly for salvation from the Lord."

(LAMENTATIONS 3: 25–26)

WHILE WE WERE TRYING to conceive and in the adoption process, I would continually pray and remind myself every morning to wait quietly, be still, hope in him, and depend on him. At this time I lived in a home that had a screened in porch that faced east. I would wake every morning to drink my coffee, watch the sunrise, and write in my prayer journal. My writing was my devotional time and my prayer time. This routine would set my day in motion and put encouragement in my heart. Every morning I had to decisively choose joy, patience, and faith.

Once my day began and I experienced earthly annoyances and inconveniences, my joy and patience would deteriorate. Heavy rains and traffic on the way to a doctor appointment where I had to sit and wait for a nurse to take my blood. Another ultrasound that showed little to no promising egg growth. Another round of hormones wreaking havoc on my body. Another negative pregnancy test to end the day. Every night I was weary of waiting and exhausted from hoping. I was also burned out from formulating my own plans to take matters into my own hands.

The next morning my day would begin as it always did, coffee, sunrise, prayer journal. And I would feel refreshed and hopeful again. Waiting quietly was a daily surrender on my part.

When you surrender you can depend on him for energy, strength, rest, and joy. Do not be discouraged when your faith waivers. Surrendering can be a daily struggle, and we have to do it repeatedly. Each time we try to control the situation and get frustrated, we are allowed to surrender again. That daily surrendering will build our hope and our dependence.

Wait with Prayer

Pick a time in your day to schedule prayer and devotional time, and mark this commitment on your calendar.

After a week, notice your energy and attitude change on days you have honored that time.

Journal about any change on days that you do not honor that commitment.

Chapter Twelve

Prune Your Fruit

"Yes, I am the vine; you are the branches. Those who remain in me,
and I in them, will produce much fruit. For apart from me
you can do nothing."

(JOHN 15:5)

I GREW UP GOING to a church every Sunday with my parents. We showed up, checked the box, and moved on to lunch and naps. My mom, my grandmother, and my aunts are all women of faith, but we didn't have many discussions around what that faith consisted of or meant besides attending church. I attended Bible schools in the summer and completed the sacraments, but I did not have a personal relationship with God. I knew him as a magical, governing, all-knowing power in everyone's lives.

It wasn't until my husband and I were struggling with infertility that I began to work on my faith life. I was broken and lost and needed hope. I started reading, praying, and journaling. We found a church that we felt comfortable in and started meeting people in real relationships with Jesus. By the time we entered the adoption process, I was learning and growing in my relationship with God through the knowledge of Jesus. I was surrounded and encouraged by people who were strong in their faith. Every decision, worry, struggle, failure, and success of the adoption process grew my faith. The timing of my faith journey was impeccable and not at all a coincidence.

Now as a parent I also experience many days that are only endured because of my growing faith. When my children were babies, I had inexplicable fear that they would become very ill or stop breathing at any minute. Sleepless nights can make a mama's thoughts irrational and unending. These nights were more opportunities for me to dig into my faith and release my worries to my Heavenly Father.

Oftentimes I become distant from my faith when I do not put in the time to grow. When I am actively present in church instead of just checking the attendance box, I feel closer to God. When I set aside time for prayer and devotion, I feel stronger in my faith. When I build relationships with others who are strong in their faith, then I notice the good fruit. I am kind. I am positive. I am patient. When I remain in my Father's love, I can do anything.

Wait with Prayer

What are you doing today to remain in a personal relationship with Jesus?

What are the distractions that leave you distant from your faith?

List the good fruits you notice when you are seeking growth.

Chapter Thirteen

Harvest Your Fruit

"But when the Holy Spirit controls our lives he will produce this kind
of fruit in us: love, joy, peace, patience, kindness, goodness,
faithfulness, gentleness, and self–control."

(GALATIANS 5:22 TLB)

EARLY ON IN OUR adoption journey while we were waiting to
be matched, I reluctantly joined a weekly Bible study at our new
church. I was not working at the time–so aside from the mounds
of adoption paperwork and meetings with social workers–my
days were mostly free and somewhat lonely. I joined a morning
Bible study advertised at my church and showed up on day one
as the youngest person in the room by about twenty-five years. I
later realized most people my age were probably working during
the morning hours and I had inadvertently joined a retiree's Bible
study. Everyone was warm and welcoming as people usually are in
the South, but I wanted to run. How would I ever connect with a
group completely out of my peer range?

But I stayed. I stayed and I learned and I received. I received
support and, most importantly, I received the Holy Spirit. My
group completed a book and study on the Holy Spirit, a topic
that besides the occasional reciting of childhood prayers, I knew

nothing about. I learned that the directional pulls I feel in my daily life are Jesus using the Holy Spirit to communicate with me. These knowledgeable and faithful ladies in my study were filled with the Holy Spirit. Not only did I learn about the Holy Spirit but I realized that the Holy Spirit is why I was sitting in this very room with these very people.

It became clear to me that the fruits of the Holy Spirit are produced in us when we use the desire God provides to seek goodness. The days that our hearts remain open to receiving love, joy, patience, kindness, goodness, faithfulness, gentleness, and self–control, are the days these fruits are waiting for us.

Can we possibly have all of this fruit at one time? And once we have all the fruit, does it ever run out? These sweet fruits are provided by a God who loves us and who prepares our hearts to receive them. The Holy Spirit taps us on the shoulder when one of these fruits is depleting. Then he whispers in our ear so that he may fill us with more.

Wait with Prayer

Which fruit are you filled with the most on a daily basis, and which fruit do you feel depleted of?

What is your most vivid experience with the Holy Spirit? These experiences can be small like the voice telling you to go back and recheck the door lock. Or these experiences can be large like the time you felt a nudge to take a different route and you missed a traffic accident or an impending disaster.

What discipline in your life helps you tune in to the Holy Spirit and the help that it provides in our life?

Chapter Fourteen

Impatiently Waiting

"Wait patiently for the Lord. Be brave and courageous.
Yes, wait patiently for the Lord."

(PSALM 27:14)

WHEN AN EXPECTANT PARENT meets with a lawyer or an agency to make an adoption plan, they are shown "profile" books of waiting adoptive couples to choose from. Once our rigorous home study was complete and our profile book was created, we were waiting every day to hear if an expectant parent had chosen us.

We were elated the first time our profile book was chosen and viewed by an expectant mother. We received a phone call from a lawyer who told us she wanted to meet with us–and two other couples. This was it! Never mind that the expectant mother was also meeting with two other adoptive couples. This was our moment. This is what every adoptive couple is waiting for. We were finally chosen.

During our meeting with the young lady, we immediately connected with her and knew she was the one for us. She was young but confident, scared but smart, and she was making a brave and definite decision to place her baby for adoption. We drove home from that meeting with smiles on our faces and hope in our hearts.

Two days later we found out that although we thought she was the one for us, we were in fact not the ones for her. She chose another couple and we were in shock. What did we do or say wrong? What could we do differently next time so that we would be chosen? We were so confident it would work out and extremely hurt and saddened that it didn't. So we began to think about the uncertainty of our future. How many times would this happen before being chosen? How many times would we be rejected? Should we pursue more options? Should we knock on more doors? Should we cast a wider net? This was going to be harder than we thought.

Our world tells us to pursue more options, keep knocking, go after our goals, and make it happen. It can be extremely puzzling to know what action to take when a door is closed. Our Heavenly Father tells us to be still, be brave, and wait patiently for him to make the way.

Wait with Prayer

List a circumstance in which you are conflicted on waiting patiently or bravely pursuing more options.

Prayerfully consider all paths and wait for a clear and peaceful direction.

Chapter Fifteen

Trust Fall to Your Knees

"Trust in the Lord with all your heart and do not lean on your own
understanding. In all your ways acknowledge him
and he will make your paths straight."

(PROVERBS 3:5–6 NASB)

OUR PROFILE BOOK WAS viewed many times after we met with the
first expectant mother who did not choose us. That was our first
rejection, but it was not our last. We received several calls with
situations that did not turn out to be our moment. Every call was a
chance to be a parent, but when the situation didn't turn out to be a
match for us we felt the loss of that opportunity. Every call brought
us through emotions of hope and expectancy—yet helplessness,
and ultimately grief.

Then in the middle of normal life on a normal day we received the phone call that ultimately made us parents. An expectant mother chose our profile and wanted to meet us. During our
meeting the very next day, the expectant mother asked if we would
parent her baby girl. This was a moment we dreamed about and
prayed for daily. You plead with God and tell him that if he could
just answer that prayer then you won't ask for anything else. However, there were seventeen more weeks of waiting and still many

prayers to be answered. God was only using the adoption process to prepare our hearts for the faith we would need while waiting for the birth of our daughter. There were so many what if moments that brought me to my knees, and every time I came up with a tear stained face and a peace that I could not understand. Every single time I acknowledged him and drew closer to him, my path was made straight.

Our minds cannot fathom what our hearts believe. If you cannot wrap your head around the vastness of God, let your heart lead when trusting and believing. Our minds are too small and too rational to understand and acknowledge God's love for us.

Wait with Prayer

What specific moments in your life have you felt divine intervention was present?

What areas in your life do you struggle handing over to God because he is not acting quickly enough?

Take this week to purposefully and prayerfully hand over those areas to God.

Use a prayer to remind yourself to release control when you find yourself taking back those burdens.

Chapter Sixteen

Dreaming of Signs

"If I had the gift of prophecy, and if I understood all of God's secret plans and possessed all knowledge, and if I had such faith that I could move mountains, but didn't love others, I would be nothing."

(1 CORINTHIANS 13:2)

THERE WAS A MOMENT in my life that I experienced a sign from God but was too human and possibly too fearful to understand. Many months before we met our daughter's birth mother, I woke from a dream with a specific date in my consciousness. I searched my life for the significance of this date but could find none. I told a few people about the experience, and made sure to write about it in my journal so that if something happened later I wouldn't question my sanity.

Nine months later on a normal weeknight, we received a call about an expectant mother who wanted to meet us. After receiving the information and discussing it, my husband and I agreed it could be the right opportunity for us. We made a plan to meet the woman the very next day. After catching my breath I realized the next day's date was April 10th. This was the date in my dream. I was doubtful of my own memory and was grateful that I thought to journal about it at the time it happened.

That dream gave me a small glimpse of the bigger picture. But because I am fearful, I doubted the subtle voice speaking to me. And I even doubted my own sanity. Did God really speak to me? Did I really have that dream? This gift should have provided faith that moved mountains. But it didn't. I was still worried with the "what if's" or "what if not's". I feared the worst, and so I made plans to protect my heart and the hearts of others around me.

But even with all of those doubts and with all of those fears, I also had love. I loved the birth mother of my daughter from the very day I met her. I loved my daughter from the very day I heard about her. Even when there is confirmation, we can have fear. Even when there is assurance, we can have doubts. But, love. Love from our Father can stand in the gap for faith until your heart catches up.

Wait with Prayer

Have you ever been given a small glimpse of God's future plan through signs or dreams?

Did this sign give you assured faith or cause you to doubt yourself?

In what way can love stand in the gap for you today?

Chapter Seventeen

Hide and Seek

"In those days when you pray, I will listen.
If you look for me wholeheartedly, you will find me."

(JEREMIAH 29: 12–13)

WE WERE MATCHED WITH our oldest daughter's birth mother when she was 17 weeks pregnant. We then waited another 17 anxious weeks until the baby was born at 34 weeks. During the wait, we dove right into a relationship with her. She was open, honest, and committed to making an adoption plan. I was in constant communication with her and I knew her every ache, craving, energy level, and life struggle. In the beginning I desired this information and our communication was ideal. As the pregnancy and our relationship progressed the communication became exhausting.

At 30 weeks, she visited the hospital every few days for contractions, pains, and general worry. I wanted to fix all her struggles and provide support but I had my own grief and fears. It all became a heavy load to carry. After each phone call or text that brought me anxiety I would immediately call my husband crying. My husband would talk me through the tears, and I would get off the phone and pray. That prayer would release all worry and take me to the next day. Every day a call. Every day worrisome tears. Every day a prayer.

Speak. He is listening. Ask. He will answer. Be still. Your Father is always working for you and with you. And when you wholeheartedly cry out to him, he is there. Know that he is always listening. You just have to ask.

Wait with Prayer

Write about a situation in your life that you approached without prayer.

Write about a situation in your life that you approached with prayer.

How were those two experiences with and without prayer different?

Chapter Eighteen

Wasting Worry

"So don't worry about tomorrow, for tomorrow will bring its own
worries. Today's trouble is enough for today."

(MATTHEW 6:34)

THE WAIT TIME BETWEEN meeting our daughter's birth mother and
her birth were filled with doctor appointments, nursery preparation, and multiple false alarm trips to the hospital. My husband,
my cousin, and I had just sat down at our favorite Mexican restaurant with margaritas, chips, and salsa when the actual labor phone
call came in. Due to multiple false alarms we decided on a plan for
the expectant mother to send us an update after she was checked
into the hospital and examined by the staff. Quickly calling for our
bill at the restaurant, we headed home to prepare for a possible stay
at the hospital.

Once we arrived home, I became overwhelmed with fear,
anxiety, and excitement. I should have packed bags and prepared
to leave but I felt paralyzed by the uncertainty of the next few moments and days ahead. I was concerned with the baby's health as
the expectant mother was only 34 weeks. I was nervous about being present for the birth and all of the emotions that the expectant
mother would be facing. I was apprehensive about the revocation

period in which the expectant mother would have five days to re-consider her decision of placing the baby in our home. So many worries of tomorrow surfaced in my head.

Meanwhile, as I was processing all of these fears, my husband laid down to take a nap. He was preparing for the most exciting time of our life by snoozing. How could he sleep at a time like this? As he lay in our bed, I irritably approached him about his choice of preparation. He calmly explained that we would most likely be up all night and into the next morning and possibly for the next few days. My husband was strategically planning for the next 24 hours. I was planning and processing worries for the next eighteen years.

I have always been a long-term planner. I worry about days, weeks, and months from now. I consider many contingency plans well ahead of time. As a result of losing ourselves in worrying for tomorrow, we lose focus on today. But I am learning that this is an area where our trust in God will provide enough energy, peace, patience, and focus for today. I once read that a day is twenty-four hours because that is all we can handle. So we know tomorrow he will provide another twenty-four hours of energy, peace, patience, and focus for tomorrow.

Wait with Prayer

Are you a long-term planner? Are you a long-term worrier?

Can you think of a time when you wasted energy and time wor-rying about a situation that turned out to be positive?

Make a habit of saying the Lord's Prayer every morning and ask-ing for your daily bread. Ask for just enough patience, energy, and strength for the upcoming day. Focus on today.

Part Three

Wait with Courage

Chapter Nineteen

Unanswered Prayers

"Always be joyful. Never stop praying. Be thankful in all circumstances, for this is God's will for you who belong to Christ Jesus."

(1 THESSALONIANS 5:16–18)

DURING MY RESEARCH ON adoption, I noticed a common theme among infertile women who adopted. These women were full of gratitude for their infertility. I struggled with the idea they were sharing, and I did not understand the magnitude of their emotion.

Then our first daughter was born and placed in our arms and lived in our home. I have a vivid memory of when that same emotion and gratitude became real for me. My daughter was only a few weeks old, and I laid her to bed after a very long day. I sat down on the couch with my husband and an overwhelming sense of grief and sadness came over me. At that very moment, I recognized that if God answered my prayers and pleading to get pregnant, then my daughter, who I loved with all my heart, would not be my daughter.

In the very first breath she took, I loved her more than I ever imagined. It baffled my mind to think that had my biggest prayers been answered, it would have meant a life without her. My life's most prevalent struggle thus far brought me to her. Now, I finally appreciate the gratitude those women have for their circumstance.

God wants us to always be thankful, every day, in all circumstances. We know that there are days when this is just downright difficult. It is on the toughest of days that you will need him the most, and on those days is when you will find him. Be thankful for difficult circumstances knowing that he is preparing you for your future, even when that future may look differently than you expected.

Wait with Courage

Have you had a circumstance or difficult time that brought you to a relationship with God?

Are you able to express praise and thankfulness in hard moments or only once the hard moment is over?

List a specific moment in life that you remember asking God, "why," only later to praise him for that very moment.

Chapter Twenty

Testing Testing

"My brethren, count it all joy when you fall into various trials,
knowing that the testing of your faith produces patience."

(JAMES 1:2–3 NKJV)

WHEN WE STARTED THE adoption process, we did a lot of research including reading books, online searches, talking to adoptive families, and educational seminars. The topic of an "interrupted adoption" was briefly discussed as a possibility. In an interrupted adoption, an adoptive family is matched with an expectant parent but that match does not result in an adoption placement. An expectant parent does not sign away parental rights until up to thirty days after the birth of the baby. Each state has its own laws on how long this "revocation period" lasts. This time period can seem brutal to an adoptive family, but it is completely necessary for an ethical adoption placement.

Our first daughter's adoption was a fairly straightforward and pleasant experience. While we were not chosen by the first expectant parent we met, we did not experience any interruptions during the first process. Our first daughter's birth mother was committed to her decision. She communicated honestly and openly in a way that helped us consider an open-adoption relationship that we had previously not considered. Although we struggled with a long wait, many unknowns, and the fear that she may reconsider, our growing relationship outweighed those fears.

When pursuing our second adoption, we experienced three interrupted adoptions in one short year that I will talk about in later chapters. Experiencing one interruption is heartbreaking and possibly expected to happen along the way. However, experiencing three interruptions in a row was an emotionally and physically exhausting experience. At times we felt hopeless and were one footstep away from giving up and walking away. Each of those trials tested our faith and our patience. Yet each of those heartaches eventually led us to our second daughter. Those trials, each one, are now counted as our joy.

Wait with Courage

List a specific trial that you have encountered that led you to a specific joy.

Journal about an experience of being in a trial and feeling utterly hopeless without being able to see past your current circumstance.

Journal about your experience of being in a trial and realizing the future outcome was going to be stronger faith and the intended path.

Chapter Twenty One

Pass it Back

"Be still, and know that I am God! I will be honored by every nation. I will be honored throughout the world."

(PSALMS 46:10)

AFTER EACH INTERRUPTED ADOPTION, I certainly thought that we were out of the valley and loss would not come again, but it did. At this point, I started to wonder if we were doing something wrong.

When pursuing adoption, there are many different resources to use, such as public agencies or private attorneys. Some of the matches we sought after were opportunities we heard about from friends or social media. Looking back on it now, we pursued a couple of situations with uncertain details that in our desperation we chose to ignore.

One situation we pursued that was unsuccessful for us was a young high school student who was being raised by her grandmother. The girl's grandmother insisted that they were not prepared to raise a baby. The family was very sweet and I remember our time together vividly. The grandmother loved her granddaughter and wanted to protect the young girl from such a challenging future. Looking back on it now, it is very clear to me that the young expectant mother had plans of her own. She communicated with us very little and most of my information came from her grand-mother. In the end the young girl came up with a plan to parent her baby on her own.

Another situation we pursued included a young mother with very little means who was pregnant with twins and already parent-ing three children. Several of her family members supported her decision to place the babies for adoption but were also willing to help the mother if she would decide to parent the twins. Although the young mother seemed overwhelmed with her situation, she seemed firm in her decision to place the babies so that she could provide for her current children. Months after she chose us to par-ent and a couple of weeks before her due date, her mother called to let us know that she would be helping the expectant mother parent the twins. The young mother now had a commitment for help and a plan to keep her family together.

I started to wonder if our emotional decisions and efforts were bringing us these losses. Were we causing this heartache and loss in our lives by making emotional decisions over rational decisions? Were we ignoring red flags? Were we trying too hard instead of waiting on God?

There is always a fine line between going after your goals, making things happen for yourself, and waiting on God. Often we work hard, fail, and then pass it back to God after we have been defeated. Sometimes it takes several defeats before we learn to step away and be still. Our Heavenly Father wants us to pursue oppor-tunities but also to seek him and know when to walk away with a lesson when he closes the door. Some seasons in life he is drawing us closer and calling for us to be still and know that he is God.

Wait with Courage

Describe a time in your life that you felt you were following the right path but continued to run into closed doors.

Describe a time in your life when a goal you pursued felt effort-less with various open doors.

What does it look like for you to "be still" and hand your defeats back to God? (prayer time, journaling, intentional rest, seeking a mentor or friend with similar experiences)

Chapter Twenty Two

Love After Loss

"Three things will last forever—faith, hope, and love—
and the greatest of these is love."

(1 CORINTHIANS 13:13)

I MENTIONED BEFORE THAT as our story unfolded, we experienced several interrupted adoptions between the birth of our first and second daughters. I will write more details on these losses in subsequent chapters, but I will summarize that challenging season here.

The first loss was the stillborn birth of a baby girl named Isabella. When our oldest daughter was 14 months old, we were matched with an expectant mother who was due in six weeks. One week before her due date we stood by her side while she experienced a late term stillbirth. We attended a memorial service with the birth family for a child we both grieved.

The second loss was a baby girl we named Evelynn. When our oldest daughter was 17 months old, we were matched with a very young expectant mother whose family was pushing her to place her unborn child. One week after we brought this baby into our home, this young mother finally got the courage to speak her choice to her family. She arrived with a tear-stained face and rightfully removed her baby from our arms.

The third and fourth loss were twin boys we named Samuel and Myles, but we never had a chance to meet. When our daughter was 24 months old, we were matched, prepared for, and expecting twin boys. Two weeks before they were born, the expectant grandmother contacted us to let us know that she would be supporting the expectant mother in parenting the boys. While we were disappointed, we were happy that this young mother found a way to keep her family together.

It was an emotionally challenging year for our hope. It was an endurance testing year for our faith. But we persevered through the year and the losses with love. After each loss my husband and I would turn towards each other with more support, more thoughtfulness, and more love. With each loss we grieved differently, but we grieved together. Everything we knew felt hard. But our love for each other felt easy. While our hope and our faith were wavering with each circumstance, our love was growing and evolving.

In addition to growth in our marriage during these challenges, we experienced changes among our family relationships and friendships. In the beginning of our trials, we had a tendency to hide the hard experiences and loss to protect others from the pain we were feeling. We quickly learned that outside of each other, we also required the love and support of family and friends. Once we started to share our pain, we were able to receive the support needed from those close to us. Love of each other and love from others helped us to feel like we were not alone in our pain. While faith and hope may waver, love from our Heavenly Father will last forever.

Wait with Courage

Have you been through a trial that pulled you away from your loved ones? Journal about that experience.

Have you been through a trial that pulled you closer to your loved ones? Journal about that experience.

Chapter Twenty Three

Hold Me

"Don't be afraid, for I am with you. Don't be discouraged, for I am
your God. I will strengthen you and help you. I will hold
you up with my victorious right hand."

(ISAIAH 41:10)

As PREVIOUSLY TOLD, OUR first adoption loss was the stillborn
birth of a baby girl named Isabella. When our oldest daughter was
one-year-old we decided it was time to pursue adoption again. We
refreshed our documents and updated our home study and were
matched within a quick few months. The expectant mother was
due with a baby girl within weeks of our match. She was alone with
minimal family support and was confident of her decision. The
match was a whirlwind experience compared to our first match
and we were elated it happened so quickly and seamlessly. We joyfully shared the news with our family and friends and prepared
our house for baby #2.

One week before the expectant mother was due; I received
a call in the early morning hours from her mother. The expectant
mother went to the hospital in severe pain, and they were unable
to find the baby's heartbeat. We were devastated for our own hearts
but more devastated for this woman. We instinctively headed to

the hospital. We were anxious and fearful and unsure of our role in this situation, but we wanted to support her.

We arrived at the hospital without a plan. My husband stayed with our toddler in the waiting room as I went to check on the expectant mother. I remember walking into her hospital room and seeing her in pain–both mentally and physically. Her pain was clearly something I had never experienced, and I didn't know the right way to support her or the right words to say. I was scared she would reject us and become angry, and I wanted to run. But I also felt a heavenly urge to go to her and be present. Within an hour of our arrival the baby was stillborn at 39 weeks. In the following days, we mourned with her and assisted her in honoring her baby.

When I remember the details of those fearful moments, I know I was being held up by my Father's hands. Without his urge and guidance, we may have run from such a painful and awkward experience. We were unsure of where to go or what to do or what to say. But we did not have to do it alone.

When fear and anxiety creep in, return your focus back to the one who promises to provide strength and help. Move forward with his urging and know that he is with you and will guide you. He will hold you up.

Wait with Courage

Journal about a fearful experience in which you know that without God's support you might have moved forward in a different way.

Chapter Twenty Four

Which Direction

"The Lord himself will fight for you. Just stay calm."

(EXODUS 14:14)

THREE MONTHS AFTER THE loss of Isabella, we were matched with a very young birth mother who chose us to parent her unborn daughter. On an icy cold day in February, we left our daughter with my mother and drove six hours to a hospital for the birth of a baby we named Evelynn. The expectant mother asked me to be with her in the delivery room along with her mother and grandmother. The moment Evelynn arrived, her young and scared birth mother grabbed my hand tightly, and with tears in her eyes she made me promise to care for her baby in a way that she could not. On the other side of the delivery room, the birth mother's family were taking in the beautiful first sights and sounds of the baby as the nurses weighed and cleaned her.

That afternoon my husband and I paced in a private hospital room waiting while the birth family spent time with Evelynn. We previously agreed on a birth plan that would have the baby sleeping in the room with us until she was discharged a few days later. That night the nurse showed up to our hospital room empty handed with news that the birth family wanted to care for the baby overnight. Over the next few days several more members of the birth family showed up to meet the baby. We spent time with several members of the birth family and the baby–carefully respecting their space.

After a couple of stressful days in the hospital, paperwork was reluctantly signed and the baby was discharged in our care. We drove home with Evelynn and over the next week we tried to settle in with a new baby and a toddler, but things just felt uneasy. After the tense hospital experience, my husband seemed disconnected and immediately dove back into work. Meanwhile, I was having a hard time bonding with Evelynn during the fearful revocation period. Throughout the week we received varying reports from our lawyer of family members trying to convince the birth mother to revoke her decision. We were on high alert which caused a lot of emotions and stress. On the early morning of the fifth and final day of the revocation period we received a call from our lawyer. The birth mother and her family were on their way to pick up the baby. The young mother officially revoked her decision to place the baby for adoption. Now what? I placed Evelynn into the crib and walked out of the nursery. I was devastated, empty, and calm as I kneeled down in prayer.

In the midst of my pain, I was reminded to stay extremely calm so that I could hear his direction better. When we panic and act out of fear we invite chaos and stress into our daily lives and daily decisions. In my state of calm I came to the realization that even though I desperately wanted a baby, in no way did I want to parent a child whose birth mother was unsure of the placement. In this desperate moment, I was reminded that although The Lord wants to fight for you, sometimes his fight does not look how you want it to look. He wants to part the sea. He wants to guide your feet. He wants to make your crooked paths straight. Stay calm and allow him to fight for you.

Wait with Courage

In what area of your life have you completely surrendered and allowed the Lord to fight for you?

Can you think of a moment when you let panic take over and possibly acted out of fear?

Can you think of a moment when you were able to focus on the Lord and stay calm?

Chapter Twenty Five

Can't Go Around It

"For you know that when your faith is tested,
your endurance has a chance to grow."

(JAMES 1:3)

AFTER A WEEK OF caring for Evelynn in our home, her mother revoked her decision to make an adoption plan. Very early in the morning, on the last day of the revocation period, I missed a call from our adoption attorney. I was still sleeping because I was up all night with an agitated newborn and a restless toddler. The attorney then called my husband at work to let him know that the birth family was already one hour into the six-hour drive to our area. My husband rushed home to break the news to me before I heard it from the lawyer, but it was too late. I had woken and immediately returned the missed call from the attorney. I hung up the phone just as he burst through our front door. Although neither of us were surprised because of the events earlier in the week and at the hospital, we were still very broken and lost as to what to do next.

We were told to make arrangements to meet and relinquish baby Evelynn, whose name was now not Evelynn, to her birth family. We sat for a moment to figure out our next steps and decide how to properly send her off to her forever family. Instead of having this painful memory tied to our home, we decided to arrange to meet them at our church. I changed her clothes and packed a few items into a small bag for her including the outfits the birth family had given to us and only one very thin blanket from our home. My husband and I arrived at our church a bit early and sat on the couch in our pastor's office with the baby swaddled on our laps. I was hurting. My husband was angry. The baby was sleeping.

Our very wise pastor acknowledged our brokenness and could sense our need to complete the surrender and move on as quickly as possible. His assessment of our feelings was right. I was ready to hand over the baby, take a step forward, and forget this ever happened. I was anxious to run from the pain as fast as I could. Instead, our pastor encouraged us to "sit in this pain" rather than push it away. He personally and professionally knew the potential for growth from pain. As I listened to his words and his prayer for us, I felt permission to grieve rather than to run.

If we give ourselves time and permission to process the pain from our losses, we then give our faith a chance to grow. Allowing ourselves to feel the pain–rather than going around it or going over it–provides endurance. Our path has to be through the pain so that the brokenness can cause new growth in our life.

Wait with Courage

Do your painful moments bring you closer in relationship to God or further away?

Are you going through the pain or around the pain?

What painful moments have you been through (instead of around) that have brought you growth?

Do you have some lingering painful moments from your past that need processing?

Chapter Twenty Six

Missing Peace

"Now we see things imperfectly, like puzzling reflections in a mirror, but then we will see everything with perfect clarity. All that I know now is partial and incomplete, but then I will know everything completely just as God now knows me completely."

(1 CORINTHIANS 13:12)

SEVERAL MONTHS AFTER THE loss of "Evelynn," we were matched with a woman who was expecting twin boys.

We met the woman and some of her family, and although they were heartbroken to place the babies, they were in support of her decision. To be honest, we were frightened with some of the details of the situation. We feared the immense responsibility as white parents raising African-American boys in a world in which they face harsh stereotypes and threats on a daily basis. We feared parenting a child whose biological sibling suffered from genetic mental disabilities leaving him nonverbal. We feared parenting twins while also parenting a toddler so close in age. In adoption the awareness of details and the undeserved opportunity to say yes or no to a situation can feel disheartening. After much consideration and many prayers we cautiously accepted the match. We moved forward joyfully sharing the news that our family was planning to grow by two.

Part Three: Wait with Courage

The expectant mother and I communicated on a limited basis for a few months as our family prepared our minds and our home for twins. A couple of weeks before her due date arrived there was a significant drop in communication on her end. I could feel her pulling away and my heart knew something was changing, but I continued on with the hope that our family was growing soon. After several failed attempts to reach her, I finally received a call from her mother whom I had never spoken to. The woman informed me that she was stepping in to help support her daughter. The woman, whom we had never met, pronounced that the expectant mother would not be following through on the adoption plan. We would not be parenting the twins. Again we were experiencing an unexpected twist in our journey in which we had no control.

While we were relieved of a number of fears, we put a lot of time into preparing, praying, and alleviating those fears. We were frustrated and depleted of emotional energy. Every interrupted adoption was bringing a loss of time and a loss of hope. I remember receiving a call from my sister who provided words to encourage me. She explained that our views in life are like peeking over a fence on our tip toes and only catching a glimpse. But our Heavenly Father has the full view. Our view is partial and incomplete. God's view is everything. When we struggle with a day, a moment, a piece of the puzzle, we can remind ourselves that our view is imperfect and unclear. As moments on our journey fit into place, our views can become more complete and clear.

Wait with Courage

Is there a piece in your life right now that feels incomplete and confusing? Pray a prayer of peace for this situation and a prayer of patience for a clearer view.

Is there a moment in your life when you finally understood a past unanswered prayer as it fit perfectly into place? Pray a prayer of praise for this unanswered prayer and for the clarity that it gave you.

Chapter Twenty Seven

Pushed Backwards

"For I know the plans I have for you," says the Lord. "They are plans for good and not for disaster, to give you a future and a hope."

(JEREMIAH 29:11)

THIS VERSE FROM JEREMIAH is frequently offered by well-meaning friends when adversity enters our lives. In the past, before facing my own particular hardships, I also provided this verse to support others. I have seen this verse used after friends have lost loved ones to disease or tragic accidents. I saw this verse posted as encouragement for my sister-in-law when she lost her baby at twenty-weeks gestation. I heard this verse and read it after every negative pregnancy test, every time a birth mother didn't choose us, and after each of the adoption losses we experienced. But these losses, these backward steps, they all felt like disaster. He promises plans for good and for a future and for hope, but in those immediate moments of loss, I did not feel hopeful at all. So what do we tell ourselves and others in the current moment of grief? Do we process failure, death, or diagnosis as the intended path? How can today's disaster turn into a good future?

Without knowing and seeing the big picture, we cannot understand the setbacks until further along the journey. This limited view can make the disastrous moments and loss in our life feel too big to overcome. With only a glimpse of the plan or a piece of the puzzle, we cannot fully grasp the future. When we are in a relationship with Jesus, we can trust that somehow this grief, this backward step, will also be used for good. God did not design the disaster, the loss, or the failure. His promise is that in relationship with him, he will get you through the hard times to reach the joyous future and hope he has for you.

Wait with Courage

List defining moments in your life when you felt like you were taking backwards steps and questioned the plan.

Have you had disastrous moments in your life that made you question him entirely?

Are you still in a season in which you are questioning his plan for a good future?

Describe a defining moment in your life that God's plan looked different than your plan and worked out for the good.

Part Four

Wait with Faith

Chapter Twenty Eight

Forget Me Not

"Then they believed his promises and sang his praise. But they soon
forgot what he had done and did not wait for his plan to unfold."

(PSALMS 106: 12–13 NIV)

AFTER OUR FIRST ADOPTION was finalized, we told anybody and
everybody our story. We shouted from the rooftops what God had
done for us. In the grocery store, on social media, on walks in our
neighborhood, and on stage at church. Our first adoption story
was so joyful and full of hope that we wanted the world to know
about it.

Our second adoption process did not go as smoothly as the
first. In 14 months we experienced the loss of three interrupted
adoptions. With every subsequent loss of that year we let pain
enter our hearts. We grew weary and failed to sing his praise. Although we had proof of God's promises waking up in a crib in our
house every morning, we let adversity steal our joy.

What we failed to realize, however, is that we also need to
share God's story in those moments of adversity. Our second
daughter was born at twenty–five weeks gestation with an unknown future and many possible medical challenges. During this
time, we found ourselves leaning heavily on our faith and God's

promises. Although our second successful adoption had challenges, it also brought a story of God's promise to share with others. He is in our joyous moments as well as our painful moments.

Oftentimes we go around telling people how good our God is, but when it comes to waiting on him we forget how good he has already been in our lives. Don't let time, pain, or grief fade the memory of what God has already done for you. Be mindful to sing his praises, not only in the joyous moments, but also sing when he is walking you through challenging times.

Wait with Faith

Remind yourself of all the good things that he has already done in your life by journaling about them.

What joyful moments and answered prayers do you acknowledge and share with others as God's work?

How comfortable are you with sharing your story and how often are you sharing?

Practice sharing your story when someone else shares theirs and then move into being the first to share.

Chapter Twenty Nine

Ask and You Shall Receive

"You haven't done this before. Ask, using my name, and you will
receive, and you will have abundant joy."

(JOHN 16:24–25)

AFTER THE THREE HEARTBREAKING losses, we were emotionally
drained and feeling that we may need to step away from the adoption process completely. Our heartache and anxiety was seeping
into our relationships and our parenting. We needed protection
for our hearts. So, instead of stepping away completely we made a
decision to put conditions in place for the next situation we would
accept. Once again in this process we were foolishly trying to take
control by having a plan.

The first condition we insisted on was that we only wanted to
be matched with a baby who was already born and not currently
in utero. We thought this condition would alleviate a significant
portion of the wait and ease preceding emotional attachment. The
second condition we decided on was to have our social worker
discern not only the commitment of the expecting parents, but
also the availability of their immediate family's help. We assumed
this condition would alleviate the risk of having a decision revoked
after placement.

For this purpose, I went to my Heavenly Father and asked for these specific prayers. Indeed, a few months later we received a phone call from our social worker about a baby who 1) was born the day before and 2) both birth parents were committed to making an adoption plan due to financial and family circumstances.

While the specific prayers we asked for were answered, we would soon need more prayers and more faith. Because what we also learned on this phone call from our social worker was that our soon-to-be second daughter was born at twenty-five weeks gestation weighing one pound and eight ounces with an unforeseen medical future. While I did not see it at the time due to cloudy visions of fears and unknowns, this was a perfect answer to my demanding requests. God wanted me to know that even with abundant joy, there is room for more prayers and more faith.

Our Heavenly Father specifically tells us to do what we haven't done before. He tells us to go to him, use his name, ask and we shall receive abundant joy. He may not answer the prayer in the way you expect. He may not answer according to your timeline. But have faith; if you ask in Jesus' name, he will answer. In his own perfect way and in his own perfect time, he will provide abundant joy. If you haven't done this before, do it now.

Wait with Faith

Have you gone to the Lord and asked him in his son's name to answer your prayer?

List a specific prayer request you asked for and received.

List a specific prayer request you have not yet asked for. Ask for that prayer request now.

Chapter Thirty

Reasons to Run

"But when I am afraid, I put my trust in you."

(PSALM 56:3)

ON NOVEMBER 3RD 2015, on a beautiful rare southern fall morning, I received a phone call about an adoption opportunity for our family. My heart leapt as the social worker explained that the birth parents of a baby born that morning were making an adoption plan, had chosen our profile, and wanted to meet us. My heart skipped as the social worker informed me of the baby's life-threatening prematurity and unknown future health conditions. The baby was born at twenty-five weeks gestation and weighed one pound eight ounces. She was born breathing on her own but quickly had to be intubated for oxygen assistance. She was stable, but she faced many unforeseen risks and would likely be hospitalized for months. We had no experience and did zero research on prematurity; however, we did check it off on our adoption paperwork as a medical concern that we would consider.

As I listened carefully to the social worker and jotted down notes, my instinct was to guard our already fragile hearts. I was fairly certain that this was not an opportunity we could consider; however, I still needed to discuss it with my husband. As I prepared to call him, I looked over my notes and thought of a million reasons to run. If we said yes to this baby, the reality was that she may not survive. I was not willing to invest my heart into a situation with this great of a risk for loss.

I called my husband and tearfully explained the situation and all the reasons we should run away. After listening to all my doubts and all my fears my husband calmly replied, "I can't think of any reason we should say no." This fearless certainty came from a man who weeks earlier admitted that after all the loss and grief we endured he was ready to give up. Weeks before he didn't want to continue to pursue adoption anymore, and I was practically in agreement. So we made a plan to limit the time and energy we invested in a situation that may not be successful. We made a plan with stipulations, rules, and criteria of what opportunities we would consider. We had a plan in place to take control. Then, our second daughter was born at twenty-five weeks gestation, fearless and beautiful and perfect in God's image.

Putting our trust in God does not always mean that there won't be worry or loss or pain in our journey. It means that we have somewhere and someone to turn to when we are afraid. It means we have someone and something to trust in.

Wait with Faith

What worry in your life have you completely handed over to God?

What worry in your life do you need to completely hand over to God?

Chapter Thirty One

Have No Fear

"Such love has no fear, because perfect love expels all fear. If we are afraid, it is for fear of punishment and this shows that we have not fully experienced his perfect love."

(1 JOHN 4:18)

I WAS OVERWHELMED BY fear when we got the call from our social worker about our second daughter. As the social worker explained the situation of extreme prematurity and unknown future medical conditions, I thought of every possible reason to run. As I sat alone and processed the information, my mind was filled with possibilities and worries. What will happen if her prematurity causes hearing loss? How will our life change if she has blindness or cerebral palsy? How will we support her in the future if she has mental or learning disabilities? How long will she be in the hospital? How would we care for a critically ill child in the NICU and a toddler at home? And in the very forefront of my mind was the question, "what if we said yes and then she didn't survive?" Everything in my heart said, "no," out of fear of another possible loss. I did not want to love her and lose her. I did not want to open ourselves to possibly more grief. With this information and opportunity, we now had to decide if we wanted to be presented as a family to the birth parents.

After sitting in this spin of possibilities and fear, I called my husband to relay the information. I was already certain that he would agree with me that the risks were far too great. But, it turns out that he did not agree. After listening to me not only relay the facts from our social worker but also the many fears I was processing, my husband confidently replied. He said that he saw absolutely no reason not to pursue this situation. My husband immediately responded to all the fears and possibilities with perfect love. And every day I am reminded of that love when I see my strong and independent daughter.

We are human and we are fearful. We go to great lengths to avoid risk and pain so much so that sometimes we miss out on joy. God promises that his perfect love can expel all fear. God's perfect love gives us a reason to risk loss with hope even in the midst of fear.

Wait with Faith

What goals or things are you avoiding because of fear? (a project, a person, a life change, a new experience)

Do the benefits of achieving those goals outweigh the fears that you have?

Are your fears reality based or are your fears perceived out of past trauma?

How can you use God's promises to overcome your fears?

Chapter Thirty Two

Set You Free

"I prayed to the Lord, and he answered me.
He freed me from all my fears."

(PSALMS 34:4)

DURING THE FIRST FEW days of my youngest daughter's stay in the NICU, the reports from the medical staff were surreal. She was born at twenty-five weeks gestation and her condition was critical. My husband and I were uneducated and unprepared for the challenges she was facing. Among the daily medical updates were reports of blood in her urine, testing for brain bleeds, a hernia that would need to be repaired before discharge, a condition called ROP that could take her sight, and more. We visited the hospital multiple times a day and phoned in every four hours for updated information and any signs of progression and growth.

The unknown territory of a child needing twenty-four hour medical support was crippling. The first few weeks we wanted every detail of her condition. One positive update would bring us joy and four hours later another negative update could bring us panic. She was expected to be in the hospital until her due date which was three months away. As we settled in for her long stay, we had to change in the way we were handling the situation. We could not endure the next few months with this much fear and uncertainty. I could not control my daughter's health and I could not function as a wife and mom to a toddler at home with so much anxiety.

When we pray, we are asking for a result or for something to happen. Or when we pray we are asking for protection or for something to not happen. There are times when our prayer request seems too large and miraculous. And there are times when our prayer request for peace will seem too vague. Our Heavenly Father accepts all prayer requests in any form, for he knows our needs before we ask him. Help me, Lord. Free me, Lord. Complete thoughts or cries for help are all prayers that are heard. If you struggle with the right words, try a simple request to be freed from fears. A freedom from fear can help us move through our situation with more courage and peace.

Wait with Faith

Are your prayers usually specific (get me this job) or general (take away this feeling)?

How can you alter your prayers from specific goals to basic requests of sustenance?

Have you ever felt an instant relief from prayer that helped you move forward in your day?

Chapter Thirty Three

Fix Your Thoughts

"You will keep in perfect peace all who trust in you,
all whose thoughts are fixed on you!"

(ISAIAH 26:3)

I QUICKLY LEARNED AFTER my daughter's birth that a baby born at twenty-five weeks gestation faces many possible health concerns. The hospital briefly educated us on the possible complications of cerebral palsy, impaired hearing and vision, chronic lung disorder, and most of all the risk of infection while in the hospital.

During my daughter's one-hundred day NICU stay, a friend of mine asked if I was doing research to identify all of the health concerns and possible treatments. My friend knew that I was the type to do my research and assumed I would want to know any and every health complication possible to prepare emotionally. I answered her question with an emphatic "no." Beyond the education and information I was getting from the hospital staff, I would not do any further research.

When we were told she had blood in her urine and then at one point she stopped urinating, I prayed. When we were told her bloodwork showed a possible infection so they started her on antibiotics, I prayed. When they told us her scans showed a slight brain bleed that would likely absorb itself, I prayed. When they told us they took her off of oxygen but she was breathing too rapidly, I prayed. When they told us she would need surgery to correct a hernia before being discharged, I prayed. When she lost a couple of ounces instead of gaining ounces, I prayed. Several times a day and for every worry, I prayed to focus on the actual situation instead of every potential possibility. Trusting in my Heavenly Father and fixing my eyes on our relationship brought me peace.

On any given day, our brains are overloaded. I have unfinished projects, unnecessary worries, contingency plans for worst-case scenarios, and a grocery list. It is hard to quiet those thoughts and settle ourselves on a daily basis. We are promised that if we fix our thoughts on the Lord he will provide us with perfect peace. Perfect peace does not mean our lists go away but it does mean we are at peace with those thoughts.

Wait with Faith

Journal about an experience in which you expected to be anxious but you instead felt perfect peace.

What actions or thoughts did you put in place to arrive at this peace?

Journal about an experience that is causing you anxiety and the action items you can put into place to find peace.

Chapter Thirty Four

Quiet Please

"Let all that I am wait quietly before God, for my hope is in him."

(PSALMS 62:5)

As I mentioned several times, our youngest daughter was born one pound eight ounces which we now know is referred to as a "micro preemie." Premature babies face possible digestive, respiratory, and infection issues. The odds of a micro preemie without minor or major health issues are very slim.

Because of life, work, and a two-year-old at home, it was impossible to stay by our fragile daughter's hospital bed twenty–four hours a day. Children under the age of twelve were not allowed in the NICU so each day we struggled to balance childcare and visits to the hospital. Some days required one of us spending one hour with the baby while the other entertained our toddler on the outdoor grounds surrounding the hospital. We were unable to hold our daughter for the first four weeks of her life which meant we were showing up just for the sight of her tiny body sleeping and growing. As time progressed and she grew stronger, we were able to hold her, change her, and feed her. Now that we were able to spend time caring for her, we alternated visits so that the other person could have an afternoon at home for rest and to spend time with our toddler.

For three months, we floated in and out as often as possible, but every night we went home to a house without a crying newborn. While it was incredibly difficult to leave her at the hospital each day, my husband and I felt inexplicable peace about her condition. Each time I had to leave her, I was confident that not only were the well-equipped and well-trained nurses and doctors looking after her, but most importantly so was my Heavenly Father. My wait and my hope that she would survive her stay and one day wake me crying in the night was in him.

When your hope is in him, waiting will look and feel different. When your hope is in him, waiting can be peaceful and joyful. The worrisome moments will still arise but you will navigate through them with a quiet and hopeful heart.

Wait with Faith

What distractions disturb your quiet wait? (Social media, TV, relationships, unsupportive friends)

Make a list of things you can focus on to help your wait be more peaceful.

Make a list of verses that you can use to choose hope in a time of worry.

Chapter Thirty Five

Habits of Faith

"Now faith is confidence in what we hope for
and assurance about what we do not see."

(HEBREWS 11:1 NIV)

WHILE WE WERE WAITING to adopt, I spent a lot of my time day-dreaming about the future–in detail. How and when would we share the news of a match with our family? Should we do a video chat or an in-person visit with a sonogram picture and balloon in hand? What would our baby look like? Would the baby be a boy or girl? Would the baby be bald headed and white or black with beautiful tight coils? What will my daily life of being a mom be like? Would I be structured in routine or would I be flexible and flowy? How would my relationship with the birth parents develop? Would we communicate consistently or would it fade over time? And most importantly, what color should we decorate the nursery? Coral and gray or green and gray?

On days when I was full of confidence for the future, my daydreams filled me with expectant joy. On days when I was doubtful of the future, my daydreams filled me with longing and grief. Most days, because I was so focused on the timing, I lost faith in the certainty that we would indeed become parents.

While waiting to adopt, there are many events taking place in the background that you do not see. You are unaware when your child is conceived. You are ignorant to the difficulties that lead to the decisions of the expectant parent(s). You are oblivious to the actions of the expectant parent(s) reaching out to family for support or to an adoption agency for help. You may not know when your profile book is being viewed and discussed. Some days you see nothing happening, but everything is happening.

We typically let our daily circumstances and what we see affect our confidence or doubt. When we cannot see things happening and working in our favor we let worry and doubt sneak into our thoughts. There are habits we can choose to put into place that can stabilize our outlook. Daily time for reading, prayer, devotion, meditation, walks, and writing can help increase our mood and our faith. Work to create the daily habits that build your faith when you feel your confidence failing because of what you cannot see.

Wait with Faith

What daily habits increase your confidence and faith?

What daily habits increase your doubt and worry?

How can you turn your days of doubt into days of confidence?

Chapter Thirty Six

Guarded Heart

"Then you will experience God's peace, which exceeds anything
we can understand. His peace will guard your hearts
and minds as you live in Christ Jesus."

(PHILIPPIANS 4:7-8)

AFTER WE WERE MATCHED with our children's birth parents, the
most frequent worry and thought that interrupted our days was,
"what if they change their mind?" While the relationship building in adoption is beautiful and necessary, it is also awkward and
exhausting. What if we invest our heart into a situation that is unsuccessful? The stress of this can cause arguments with spouses,
mental exhaustion, and physical ache. I quickly learned that the
only way to survive the wait would be to surrender that thought
daily to my Heavenly Father. Each time that thought came my way,
I had to choose to entertain it or surrender it–every day.

We were matched with our oldest daughter's birth mother
when she was 17 weeks pregnant. Because this was our first match,
we didn't realize how long this would make our wait feel. I invested
a lot of time and energy into the relationship hoping that this would
help solidify her decision. She invested a lot of time and energy
reassuring me that placing her child for adoption with our family

was the best decision for her. Our first daughter's birth mother was open and honest and became part of our family. I wouldn't trade an ounce of energy for the relationship we have today.

We also had numerous situations in which we put in the time, energy, and love and the expectant parent decided not to place their child with us. We spent a lot of time not only building a relationship with one woman but also with her family. We drove hours to meet them and we supported them for days at the hospital. I was present in the delivery room and held the mother's hand for the birth of the baby. We gave them space when they needed it and we bought them dinner when they were hungry. But in the end, it was the expectant mother's right and decision to parent her child. Although this decision, and any of the expectant parent's decisions, had nothing to do with us or what we were putting into the relationship, I do know that we served a role in this family's life.

During the stressful and all consuming "waits" in our lives we can choose to surrender our worry. God promises to guard our hearts and our minds if we allow him to do so. At the time the expectant mother revoked her decision, we felt angry and sad. Once we were able to process the situation and surrender our anger, we could feel the heavy struggle and worry being lifted and replaced with a peace that cannot be described. You can walk daily knowing that if you turn it over to him, then he will guard your heart from unnecessary worry.

Wait with Faith

Have you ever been completely consumed with stress and anxiety over a circumstance yet felt that indescribable peace after consulting with God?

Try to describe that peace now through words, a song, a Bible verse, a picture.

Do you currently have a reoccurring worry that needs to be surrendered?

Pray about that worry and surrender it now.

Part Five

Wait with Peace

Chapter Thirty Seven

Modern Day Testimony

"So faith comes from hearing, that is,
hearing the Good News about Christ."

(ROMANS 10:17)

I LOVE HEARING PEOPLE'S stories of why they began their search for God and how they began to seek a personal relationship with Jesus. I was raised in a Christian family. We went to church every Sunday and I assumed God was our strength but I never thought about what that meant.

I began to seek a personal relationship with my Heavenly Father during our struggle with infertility. I dug deeper into that relationship when we entered the adoption process. I needed his comfort when we experienced the shock of an infertility diagnosis and the failure of medical intervention. I needed his proclamation of my worthiness when we heard the rejection of an expectant mother. I needed his assurance of peace when we felt the grief of a mother and her stillborn child. I needed his promise for a future when we processed the heartbreak of an interrupted adoption. Once we were able to recognize answered prayers, comprehend unanswered prayers, and rejoice in his journey, we began to appreciate the good news.

To fuel our faith, we are often pointed to the Bible to hear the Good News and God's promises. However, seeking and learning of modern-day testimonies from strangers, friends, or family can feel more relatable. Hearing someone's story can initiate, renew, transform, or grow our faith. Using the Good News of our day through sharing personal testimonies can encourage others to seek the Good News of Jesus' day. Then, reading scripture and hearing the testimony of those alive during Jesus's day becomes our priority for learning more.

Wait with Peace

What is your favorite story in the Bible?

What is your favorite testimonial from a personal friend?

If you have a testimony or story, write it here.

Chapter Thirty Eight

Commuter Prayers

"And the Holy Spirit helps us in our weakness. For example, we don't know what God wants us to pray for. But the Holy Spirit prays for us with groanings that cannot be expressed in words."

(ROMANS 8:26)

MY HUSBAND ONCE TOLD me that he is not comfortable praying and that he does not know how to pray. Frequently after his commute to or from work, he will talk to me about what he was thinking about during the drive. The thoughts he shares are usually reflective, grateful, hopeful, and emotional. One day after sharing his commuter thoughts with me for discussion he said, "I think this is the closest I get to praying." Those commuter thoughts were not close to praying. Those commuter thoughts were his prayers.

Once a week I feel the need to go on a longer run than I normally do. When I do this run my initial thoughts are on my legs, my pace, the music, and the scenery. After my body is warmed up, my thoughts always turn to people in my life and recent conversations I've had. Nearing the halfway point of my run, my thoughts transition into prayers. I have started calling this my therapy run or my prayer run.

You do not need to be in church or in your home on your knees with a well-scripted prayer to be heard. There are moments in our lives when our prayers sound like a mumbled mess or just a pouring out of our feelings. Our Heavenly Father is always listening regardless of the location and regardless of the script. Our jumbled thoughts, our cries of his name, our commute thoughts, all sound like music to his ears.

Wait with Peace

What does your prayer time look like? (routine devotion time, cries of desperation in a time of need, deep thoughts while walking or running)

What moments in your day have you looked past and not realized that you are praying? (commuting to work, writing or reading, meditative walk)

What moments in your day could you rework into prayer time? (a cup of coffee and a chat with a friend, Bible study, shower, or bath time)

Chapter Thirty Nine

Unconventional Relationships

"Now all glory to God, who is able, through his mighty power
at work within us, to accomplish infinitely
more than we might ask or think."

(EPHESIANS 3:20)

THE NUMBER ONE QUESTION we get as adoptive parents is, "do you
know your daughters' birth parents?" When we say yes people are
very curious. They want to know the details. They say we are amazing. They comment on our strength. They don't think they could
ever navigate such an uncomfortable and complicated relationship.
We are not amazing or strong, yes it is a complicated relationship,
and no the birth parents cannot revoke their final decision. We
also had some of these thoughts before experiencing the love of
God through this connection.

In those moments when we met our children's birth parents
it was both awkward and one of the most exciting moments of our
lives. These moments were also awkward and full of anxiety for our
children's birth parents. They found themselves in an agonizing situation in which they had to choose parents for their children. But our
God met us all in those anxious moments. He held our hands and
walked us through. He put us together. He built our family.

We are cautious about the information we share since the personal details of the stories are private and belong to our daughters and their birth families. Today we have different open relationships with each of our children's birth parents through email, text, and visits. Our communication and our relationships change with every season of our life and every season of their birth parents' lives. God opened our eyes to see the love of a parent from a different angle. He showed us the sacrifice that parents choose when they put their children's needs before their own. What God does to our hearts through these children and their birth parents could not be accomplished without him. He worked within us to calm our fears so that we can continue to stay connected and grow in relationship.

These relationships are not easy to navigate, but these relationships are not about us. These relationships are about our children and what is best for them. And most of all, these relationships are about the power of God to work within us all.

As individuals, we are capable of way less than if we team up with our Heavenly Father and let him work within us. If we create our relationships in him, we are capable of immeasurably more than without him. Hard things. Uncomfortable things. Great things.

Wait with Peace

Name an uncomfortable conversation, task, or visit that you have been putting off.

Pray about that specific task and set a time to accomplish it.

Once that task is completed, come back and journal about your experience. Was it positive or negative?

Did God change your heart? Did you learn anything?

How will this uncomfortable experience change you going forward?

Chapter Forty

Today's Bread

"Do not be like them, for your Father knows what you need before
you ask him. This, then, is how you should pray: Our Father in
heaven, hallowed be your name, your kingdom come, your will be
done, on earth as it is in heaven. Give us today our daily bread.
And forgive us our debts, as we also have forgiven our debtors.
And lead us not into temptation, but deliver us from the evil one."

(MATTHEW 6: 8–13 NIV)

As a child, the first prayer I learned from memory was the Lord's
Prayer. I would recite it in church every Sunday and every night
as I fell asleep. It became habitual and the words were repeatedly
rehearsed until they held no meaning for me personally.

Several years ago, I was watching a devotional video and the
author was interpreting The Lord's Prayer. She caught my attention
when she focused on the line written, "give us our daily bread." She
explains that we are asking God to give us whatever it is we need to
survive the day ahead. That daily bread could be physical strength,
rest, health, healing, money, energy, or patience. Some days we
may not know what the bread is for that day but our Heavenly
Father knows.

The Lord's Prayer is now my cry first thing in the morning. I am currently a stay-at-home mom of two beautiful, vivacious, and challenging little girls. Every morning and sometimes several times throughout the day, I ask for my daily bread–which is usually energy or patience. I now pray the Lord's Prayer with much more meaning than when I recited it as a child.

An occasional prayer will not cover our needs. We need God every day. And he is available every day. Some days we don't pray because we are lost for words or can't organize the thoughts in our head. The Lord's Prayer can help us when we cannot form the words or prayers to express our praise or our needs. Daily prayer time can help set the tone and attitude for our day.

Wait with Peace

Do you have a daily discipline involving prayer or devotional time? What does that include?

What effects does a daily prayer life have on your attitude and reactions?

Perhaps you don't know where to start. If you feel lost or uncomfortable, begin with the Lord's Prayer.

Chapter Forty One

Avoiding Major Roadblocks

"Keep on asking, and you will receive what you ask for.
Keep on seeking, and you will find. Keep on knocking,
and the door will be opened for you."

(MATHEW 7:7)

EACH TIME I AM struggling with an important decision, I consult my Heavenly Father through prayer. I have learned to ask God that if my decision is the path he wants me to choose, to then make that path void of any major roadblocks.

When my children were three-years-old and one-year-old, my husband, and I boldly moved our family across the country from our known support system. We made the choice to fulfill our personal desire to live in a location we loved, although that location is far away from family. It was a difficult decision with many moving parts and logistical steps to complete the process. At one point it looked like a previously open door would be shut, and we accepted that. However, before we had the chance to accept the closure, the opportunity immediately reopened and we resumed our previous path to relocate.

When you approach an obvious roadblock, carefully consider if there is a natural path around, over, or under that roadblock. In our situation, we kept on asking and knocking until a door was either completely closed or until our goal was accomplished. Of course, we experienced a few inconveniences like an unexpected sixteen-hour travel day and our house staying unsold for months. But inconveniences are not the same as clear roadblocks, and they should be expected.

Not only was our path void of any major roadblocks, it was incredibly blessed with encouragement. We found the perfect, fully furnished, short-term rental in the perfect location at the perfect time. There were several forks in the road and decisions to be considered, but there were also many signs of divine reassurance.

The morning after we survived our long travel day to our new location, I stumbled downstairs to get coffee and found a package on the doorstep. A friend that I hadn't seen in over ten years happened to live nearby, and she stopped by to drop off breakfast. When I stepped outside to grab the package, I heard sounds of several playful voices. With sleepy but happy eyes, I saw a young family with three girls near the same age as my daughters loading into their car. This family lived right next door and we are friends to this day.

On days when you feel depleted of all your hope and of all your energy, you will need to keep on asking, seeking, and knocking. He will answer and you will receive. Rest in that promise and be encouraged to keep on.

Wait with Peace

What important decisions or forks in the road have you consulted God on in the past?

Do you remember the path to be clearly marked and doors to be completely opened?

Do you remember a time when you made a decision that was possibly not in God's favor by evidence of roadblocks and closed doors?

Did you continue to pursue that path and have a negative outcome or did you walk away?

Chapter Forty Two

Rear-View Faith

"We do this by keeping our eyes on Jesus,
the champion who initiates and perfects our faith."

(HEBREWS 12:2A)

AFTER THE BIRTH OF our first daughter, I eagerly shared our adoption story and God's faithfulness with everyone who would listen. I shared the news of answered promises to friends and strangers. I made heartfelt posts on social media. At our church's request, I was delighted to get on stage and share with the congregation. And when our adoption agency asked, I jumped at the chance to meet with waiting adoptive families and share our story with them.

As the adrenaline wore off and the sleepless nights and exhaustion of parenting set in, I became less likely to take the time to praise him. As a scared, unconfident, and tired new parent, some days seemed longer and harder than I ever expected. Other responsibilities were requiring much of my focus and consequently, my prayer and journal time were fading away. My priorities were shifting and my gaze was no longer on the one who perfected my faith.

After the miraculous and healthy survival of our second daughter born at twenty–five weeks gestation, my gaze was realigned and my fire was refueled. I turned again to my faith to get through the days when I wasn't sure of my daughter's medical future. Once more in my time of need, I cried out in prayer, sought scripture for encouragement, and processed my thoughts through journaling. I released my worries to the one above who answered my promises for a family.

If we fail to focus on Jesus and what he teaches us, then we fail to walk forward. When we lose our focus it is like either being stuck in one spot on our journey or taking a few steps back. When our efforts falter out of circumstance, our Heavenly Father will initiate again and wait for our response. He never tires of pursuing us when we lose our way. Our circumstances and our needs should not be the driving force behind our prayer life. Reaching out for help under circumstances of need is only a piece of the relationship. We should also ask for encouragement in the mundane moments and share our praise in the joyful moments.

Wait with Peace

How do you keep your eyes on Jesus and fuel your fire of faith? (prayer time, church, Bible study, journaling)

What specific things get in the way of your focus? (exhaustion, TV, faithless friends, social media, etc.)

Make a plan to rid your days of the things that take your focus and replace them with the things that fuel your focus.

Chapter Forty Three

Dig Deep Roots

"Then Christ will make his home in your hearts as you trust in him.
Your roots will grow down into God's love and keep you strong.
And may you have the power to understand, as all God's people
should, how wide, how long, how high, and how deep his love is.
May you experience the love of Christ, though it is too great to
understand fully. Then you will be made complete with
all the fullness of life and power that comes from God."

(EPHESIANS 3:17–19)

I STRUGGLE IN MY belief. My heart is all in and fully believes that
God is my refuge. However, my head is full of questions of how
God actually exists and created the heavens. Once I heard a sermon given by a pastor who acknowledged how difficult it is for
some people to understand and believe in God. Finally! Hearing
a clergyman admit how mind baffling it can be to wrap our head
around this concept, helped me accept my struggle. This pastor suggested that we take whatever it is about Jesus that we can
understand and start from there. So I understand that Jesus is a
historical figure who was a carpenter and loved all people. So I
decided to start there. Now, I can learn more about Jesus in the
human form as a historical figure and grow from there.

My faith journey is only beginning. When I experienced God speaking to me, it seemed unfathomable since I still have so many questions. When I felt called to write this devotion, I felt unworthy since I still have moments of doubt. How am I to lift others up through scripture and prayer when I do not have all the knowledge of a scholar? Clearly, it is not about me. My words, my prayers, my experiences are about my growing faith and developing trust of God's love and promises.

God's existence, power, presence, and deep love for us is too great to understand. I have so many questions, doubts, and struggles. But I am learning that a better understanding of Jesus's teachings can lead us to accept more about God as proclaimed. The more we grow our relationship with Jesus and trust in him the deeper our roots grow in his love. Deeper roots result in a fullness of life and peace in circumstances that we can't fully understand.

Wait with Peace

What reoccurring questions or doubts surface often in your faith journey?

Have you had a circumstance or event in your life that confirmed God's presence for you?

How do you personally come to peace with a power and love so big it surpasses our understanding?

Part Six

Wait with Joy

Chapter Forty Four

Joyful Songs

"He will take delight in you with gladness. With his love, he will calm all your fears. He will rejoice over you with joyful songs."

(ZEPHANIAH 3:17B)

I AM A PLANNER. I like to have a plan for every scenario. I like to have all of my fears addressed and a contingency plan for each worst-case scenario.

I can imagine my Heavenly Father was highly amused when a planner like myself started the adoption process. There are so many questions, directions, and choices on this journey. Some of the hardest decisions for us were putting limits around possible medical diagnosis, deciding if it was right for our family to be open to any race, and determining the level of interaction we wanted with the birth parents.

Before we were informed, we decided on a closed adoption without any contact with the birth parents. Once we were educated by our agency on the benefits of open adoption for our children, we cautiously opened our hearts. We now have relationships with both our children's birth parents.

When we had to check boxes of possible medical diagnoses that we would accept, we stuck to the diagnoses we were familiar and comfortable with. In spite of our set restrictions, we found ourselves more accepting once the actual conditions were not just on paper anymore. Both of our children were born prematurely with significant hospital stays and medical risks.

And when we were asked to specify which races we would accept, we paused. We were apprehensive about our family and community's acceptance of children of a different race than our own. We wanted to make the best possible decision for the child, but we didn't know what that decision was. When actual opportunities arose, our heart and our faith took over. We now raise two children of various mixed races and ethnicities.

We tried to make these decisions and put limits on ourselves without knowing that the experience would grow us and change those decisions for us. Filling out forms and forced decisions are done with our head, but actual parenting is done with our heart. We underestimated that adoption education and faith would take over our concerns and meet our fears. It is not that we changed our minds but that the process and our faith changed our hearts.

The energy I was exerting trying to make a plan to eliminate my fears was quite laughable to God–I imagine. When I finally submitted to him and released my fears, one by one, he was so delighted that we both rejoiced in joyful songs and relief. The Lord is rejoicing in your willingness to bring him all the fears your mind could possibly imagine. And with his love, he will calm every single fear.

Wait with Joy

List your top three fears on any given day. (these can be large fears or smaller daily situations that you avoid because they make you uncomfortable)

Choose one of those fears and find a way to put yourself in a situation to face that fear. (for example, I have a fear of driving in unfamiliar places so I will plan a trip somewhere new)

Before you purposefully face that fear, pray about it and make a plan to calmly release that fear to God, and trust in him to guide you through. Then journal about your experience.

Chapter Forty Five

Different Strokes

"Don't copy the behavior and customs of this world, but be a new and different person with a fresh newness in all you do and think."

(ROMANS 12:2A TLB)

BEFORE OUR GIRLS WERE born, my husband and I were looking for a church, and we stumbled upon a pastor who spoke directly to our hearts. One of the first sermons we heard him give was titled "That's Weird and That's Good". He spoke about how being different can be good. He spoke about the challenge we face as individuals to share our faith with others and not be judged. He spoke about being bold enough to share anyway.

As individuals and a couple, we work hard at being confident in who we are. We fight the urge to fit in and conform to the ways of the world. After we adopted our daughters, this awareness became more important to us. We aim to raise our children knowing that following and imitating others is not usually the best road to take. We want them to be leaders and be themselves. As a transracial family, the push to accept and love our differences becomes even more relevant. Since we are different races than our children, we stand out and people in our community have a tendency to notice us and remember us. We can use this difference to set us apart as individuals. We can also use the recognition to be bold and share our story with others.

Resist the urge to compare yourselves to others. Our world of increasing social media outlets encourages comparison and draws us into feeling either less than or more than others. Our Father wants us to be unique. You are the only you he has made or will ever make. Rejoice! You are new. You are different. And you are you.

Wait with Joy

How much time do you spend on social media and how does it make you feel about your life?

Take a moment to clean out your social media feed so that the things you are seeing are things that inspire you.

Prayerfully consider taking a social media detox. Plan a different activity (writing, reading, walking, yoga) during the times you would normally be browsing social media. Journal about your attitude during and after the detox.

Chapter Forty Six

Social Media Update

"Be still in the presence of the Lord, and wait patiently for him to act."

(PSALM 37:7A)

SOMEWHERE IN THE MIDDLE of trying to conceive and waiting to adopt, I let social media start to affect me in a negative way. Because we felt the need to keep the details of our journey private, I felt there was nothing to share. I didn't have a positive pregnancy test with exciting news to announce. I didn't have that first family picture in the hospital bed with tired eyes and a glowing smile. I didn't have a cute baby showing growth month by month, but everyone I was friends with on social media had these desires in my heart and shared them every day.

I sat in that negative space fueling my sadness and frustration for some time. Scrolling through each picture with judgement and reading comments with a critical eye. And then I realized the negative energy I was summoning was under my control. I could choose to step away from these negative thoughts and social media. It was robbing me of, not only my joy, but also leisure time that I could spend writing, praying, and waiting patiently.

Even after becoming a parent myself and having hospital experiences with my children, I am still triggered by particular things I may have missed. Adoptive moms sometimes don't get to enjoy baby showers, gender- reveal parties, announcing and sharing the sonogram pictures, pregnancy, or even breastfeeding. I know that my particular trigger is that first family hospital picture which is most often posted on social media. To this very day, I cannot look at a picture of a mother in the hospital bed with the family gathered around welcoming a new baby without aching in my heart. I am not embarrassed of this feeling and do not hide it anymore. Give yourself permission to skip your cousin's third baby shower or to block a particular person on social media. Knowing what your triggers are and avoiding them can help your wait be less hurtful and more faithful.

In our fast-paced world with various social media outlets, we see every person's thoughts and details of their day. Search your heart for what encourages you and search your heart for what troubles you. Take action to include more encouragement and less pain in your daily life. Although rest, stillness, and even privacy are not valued or encouraged, we can choose these things for ourselves. Our Heavenly Father values our stillness and will provide whatever we need in the moment we come to him and actively rest in his love and his promises.

Wait with Joy

In this season, identify your sorrow triggers. Make a plan to remove these from your life at this time. (hospital pictures, baby showers, baby belly updates, pregnancy announcements)

How much time are you putting aside for rest and reflection?

Add into your weekly plan a specific time to actively "be still" in the presence of the Lord.

Chapter Forty Seven

Rest to the Weary

"For I have given rest to the weary and joy to the sorrowing."

(JEREMIAH 31:25)

SOMETIMES IN THIS FAST-PACED and competitive world I feel idle. My family spends a lot of time at home and we enjoy a required daily quiet time. We enjoy hiking and biking in our neighborhood, but you won't find us running around on weekends to festivals and birthday parties. Our children are not involved in any sports, dance, or music lessons. I avoid Pinterest at the cost of feeling inadequate and downright lazy. Anything beyond the daily chores, errands, school drop off and pickup, meal prep and clean up, and a few social activities is too much to ask for our family.

I grew up in the heat and humidity of Southern Louisiana where days consisted of popsicles, pools, and air conditioners. Fourteen years ago I moved to California to work in the middle of San Francisco's financial district. The entrance to the thirty-fifth-floor building was grandiose and filled with the noise of expensive shoes quickly making their way to their offices. Each day in the elevator the same conversation would play out, "Hi, how are you?"–used for small talk, not actual concern. The answer would always be an expression of how incredibly busy and overwhelmed the person had been. The busier you were at this company, in this building, in this city, the more important you were. It was an endless competition of who could fit more into their twenty–four-hour schedule.

I now see another version of this in my daily life as a stay-at–home mom. The busier mom is viewed as the more successful and more important mom. We also pass it on to our children at a very young age. They feel the need to be involved in numerous afterschool activities and attend endless social events. Our society glorifies busy over rest.

We are busy and we are weary. We need a break from our mind's running thoughts and numerous contingency plans. We need a reprieve from society's expectations of our daily activities. Taking mental and physical rest can be hard to fit into our days. Sometimes it is possible to fit but we feel shameful, lazy, or bored when we are idle. Listen to God's words and put more value on stillness. Let us clear our calendars and make space for a time of rest.

Wait with Joy

How committed is your calendar?

Are there things on your schedule that can be moved, done less often, or even eliminated?

What would a moment of daily rest look like for you? (a nap, a walk, snuggling with a child, time with a friend)

Plan an hour, a day, or a weekend of rest. Put it on the calendar and commit.

Chapter Forty Eight

Radiant Light

"Those who look to him for help will be radiant with joy;
no shadow of shame will darken their faces."

(PSALMS 34:5)

IN THE LAST FEW years I have connected with many adoptive
families in person and through social media. I have listened to
their stories of fear, loss, hope, and joy. Every one of these stories
includes prayers to God in their daily struggles and glory to God
for guidance and grace. Many times I notice that the harder the
journey and the more loss experienced, the more that person or
family will shine.

I know adoptive families who have repainted nurseries
varying shades of pink and blue to finally land back on pink. I
know adoptive families who have parented babies they thought
were long term but in the end were only there for a week. I know
adoptive families who have prepared their hearts and homes for
twins and triplets who never joined their family. I know adoptive
families who have happily drained their savings to support birth
families that ultimately chose parenting over an adoption plan. I
know adoptive families who have weaned babies from addictions
at birth.

Adoptive families and birth families will need support from their own families and their Heavenly Father. Hardships and adversity provide an opportunity to grow and become resilient. Those who have grown through hardships have a different perspective on daily struggles and inconveniences. They are able to learn that growing through seasons will provide muscle memory for years to come. Knowing how to ask for help and who to ask for help is the gift of growth. Those who need divine help and choose to seek divine help appear to radiate. All of the tears and heartache of whatever they walked through gets reflected back to others as a shining light of love and joy.

Wait with Joy

Is there a person in your life who seems to radiate light and joy?

Do they have a relationship with God?

Have they walked through a hard time in their life?

If you don't know their story, ask them to share it with you.

Chapter Forty Nine

Waste Not, Want Not

"When they had all had enough to eat, he said to his disciples,
'Gather the pieces that are left over. Let nothing be wasted.' So they
gathered them and filled twelve baskets with the pieces of the five
barley loaves left over by those who had eaten."

(JOHN 6:12–13 NIV)

IN 2010 WE EXPECTANTLY started the process of building our family by trying to conceive. In 2011 we optimistically sought help through infertility treatments. In 2012 we joyfully moved onto the adoption process. From 2012 through 2016 we were actively building our family through adoption. For six years we experienced a waiting season filled with fears, doubts, tears, prayers (answered and unanswered), heartache, joys, and growth. Not one piece of that journey was wasted. There was a purpose in each and every decision, twist, and turn.

A month after we brought "baby Evelynn" (read her story in chapter twenty four) back to her birth family, I was sitting on my front porch rehashing all the energy we had put into this particular situation, and I wrote the following in my journal:

Waste Not, Want Not

March 24, 2015

"One month ago, we showed up and prepared for the birth of a baby we thought would join our family. One month ago we showed up and gave energy, patience, worry, tears, joy, love, grace, and time. We bonded with the baby's family. We laughed with them and we cried with them. We made promises we knew we would keep. They made promises too. And then it was time. I stood right there with the expectant mother squeezing her hand and whispering encouraging words while this beautiful and perfect baby girl made her way into our world. She took her first breath, while we all held ours. I stayed and held this young mother's hands as she looked up at me weeping and managed to mouth the words, "thank you."

The details that follow are vivid and blurry at the same time. We announced the baby's arrival, her health, and her stats to our family. We celebrated through texts and phone calls. The family of the young mother showed up, held the baby, fed her, and loved her. In our hearts we knew that instead of saying goodbye, they were saying hello. We worried but we prayed and we asked others to pray. We honored our first promise to give them as much time as they needed. And we waited. We spent some time with the family and the baby. And we bonded with them some more. And we waited some more. Finally it was time to say our goodbyes. We hugged them, cried with them, and told them they were our family too. Then we sat in a cold hospital room and waited for them to say their final goodbyes to the baby. And we waited some more.

The baby was brought to us with news that the family struggled to sign the adoption paperwork. We quickly brought the baby home with pain and fear in our hearts. We half breathed. We half loved. We feared that this child may not actually be in God's plan for our family although we wanted her to be. We pretended to be mom, dad, sister, and grandma for five days until the news came. Now it was our turn to say goodbye to the baby. Now we are tired and we are heartbroken and we are angry and we are done. Someone please remove this baby from my arms. Please take her. She's not ours. As much as we want her to be she is

*not. However, she is still part of the journey. She is a piece
of us and the big picture we do not know yet.*

*And I wonder daily, "why?" Why the time, patience,
energy, joy, heartache, and tears? Why is she a piece of us?*

Our Heavenly Father promises that not one moment in our
lives whether it be heartache or joy will be of waste. He may use a
portion of your journey as growth for you or as a teaching moment
for others. One crumb of your journey could be gathered to fill
twelve other baskets. He wants you to spread the Good News and
glorify him.

Wait with Joy

Up to this point on your journey, would you look back and wish
for one piece to be removed from your path? Journal about
this piece and whether you think it was a waste or not.

Do you have a moment in your journey that you feel called to
share with others? (can you fill more baskets?)

What are ways you can use your experience to inspire others?
Your story is worth sharing.

Chapter Fifty

All God's People Said Amen

"For all of God's promises have been fulfilled in Christ with
a resounding 'Yes!' And through Christ, our 'Amen'
(which means 'Yes') ascends to God for his glory."

(2 CORINTHIANS 1:20)

EACH AND EVERY TIME a door is shut, a plan fails, and a question is answered in the negative, we take notice. Our faith will waver and our anticipation will increase. On the path to building our family we heard, "no, you are not pregnant," "no, you are not the family she chose," "no, this is not the right situation." On the path, we heard no, maybe, and not yet. But then, we heard yes. Then after another year of difficult challenges we heard yes again.

Our two daughters are our "yeses" from God. I now recognize the alternate answers had a purpose in the pain. The partial glimpse I was getting is nothing compared to the whole view that he had intended. My doubts are many and my faith wavers from day to day. My questions are endless. But every morning I wake up to my two energetic, challenging, and joyful "yeses" and that is worth all the waiting and deserves all the Amen.

God's promises in our life will appear differently than we expect. God always fulfills his promises in his way and according to his time, not ours. This variation can be challenging to accept with the limited view we have. Once our view is expanded and the picture becomes clear, we will give glory for his resounding yes. Let's not only take notice of the no's, but more importantly let us give glory for the yeses.

Wait with Joy

List your "yes" from God.

List your most painful "no," "not yet" or "not right now".

Do you have a fulfilled promise that looks slightly or completely different than you expected?

How do you or how will you glorify God for the "yes?"

Chapter Fifty One

Plant Seeds

"But the wisdom from above is first of all pure. It is also peace loving, gentle at all times, and willing to yield to others. It is full of mercy and the fruit of good deeds. It shows no favoritism and is always sincere. And those who are peacemakers will plant seeds of peace and reap a harvest of righteousness."

(JAMES 3:17–18)

MANY TIMES WHILE WRITING this devotion I struggled with the question, "who am I?" Who am I to write a devotion? Am I fit to quote Bible scripture and talk about praying and relationships with God? I have so many doubts and questions. I have never read the Bible in its entirety. My prayer life is intermittent and my relationship with God is relatively new. My journey is still unfolding and my faith is still changing and growing.

But then I heard a sermon that answered some of these questions and encouraged me. The sermon spoke about our common and daily feelings of not being enough. The sermon addressed our thoughts of feeling unqualified to complete a desire in our hearts. What makes us qualified? Who qualifies us?

Our Heavenly Father's wisdom is all knowing and all encompassing. He sincerely qualifies us when he uniquely creates us. Every one of us as a child of God is qualified to plant a seed. Every one of us is qualified to reap the harvest. Every one of us is qualified to have and build a relationship with our Heavenly Father. Even if you haven't read the entire Bible. Even if you are new in your walk of faith. Even when you fall. Even after you get back up. You are enough on day one because he is enough. You are qualified.

What are you hesitating to do or accomplish because you don't feel qualified?

You, my friend, are qualified to create.

You, my friend, are qualified by your creator.

Don't wait.

Start now.